USEFUL EXPRESSIONS

in GERMAN

FOR THE ENGLISH-SPEAKING TOURIST

Editors: A. Z. Stern — Joseph A. Reif, Ph.D.

 ·K·U·P·E·R·A·

© 1991 KS-JM Books

Distributed in the United Kingdom by:
Kuperard (London) Ltd.
30 Cliff Road
London NW1 9AG

ISBN 1-870668-69-3

INTRODUCTION

This booklet is an up-to-date and practical phrase book for your trip to Germany, Austria, or other country in which German is a second language. It includes the phrases and vocabulary you will need in most of the situations in which you will find yourself, and it contains a pronunciation guide for all the material. Some of the phrases occur in more than one section so that you do not have to turn pages back and forth. At the beginning is a basic, general vocabulary with which you should become familiar, and at the end is a list of emergency expressions for quick reference.

The pronunciation of German is fairly simple. With one or two exceptions the sounds are very similar to English sounds, and you will quickly achieve an easily understandable accent. The transcription may be read as though it were English, but attention should be paid to the following:

VOWELS:	**ah**	like **a** in father
	ei	as in height
	eh	like **e** in bed
	ew	like **ee**, but with rounded lips
	o	as in **for**
	oo	as in food
	u	like **oo** in book

CONSONANTS:		b, d, f, h, k, l, m, n, p, s, t, v, x, y, z, sh as in English
	g	as in go (not as in gentle)
	kh	has two pronunciations: (1) after **a, o, oo,** and **ow** like the **ch** in Scottish lo**ch**, (2) after other vowels, after consonants, and at the beginning of words it is pronounced more like **sh**
	r	is rolled in the back of the mouth.
	ts	occurs often at the beginning of words.

Stressed syllables are printed in **boldface.**

CONTENTS

BASIC DICTIONARY	GRUNDWÖRTERLEXIKON	GRUNT-VERTER-LEXIKON
Thank you	Danke	**dahn**ke
Thank you very much	Danke sehr	**dahn**ke zayer
Please	Bitte	**bitte**
Excuse me	Verzeihung, Entschuldigung	fer**tsei**-ung, ent**shul**digung
Never mind	Macht nichts	makht nikts
What? What is that?	Wie bitte? Was ist das?	vee **bitt**e? vahss ist dahss?
Where? Where is that?	Wo? Wo ist das?	voh? voh ist dahss?
When? How?	Wann? Wie?	vahn? vee?
Which? Why?	Welche(r)? Warum?	**vel**kher? vah**room?**
Is that?	Ist das?	ist dahss?
That is not	Das ist nicht	dahss ist nikht
Yes, no, perhaps	Ja, nein, vielleicht	yah, nein, fee**leikht**
Correct, incorrect	Richtig, falsch	**rikh**tikh, fahlsh
So so	So	zoh
Good, bad	Gut, schlecht	goot, shlekht
No good, not bad	Nicht gut, nicht schlecht	nikht goot, nikht shlekht
There is, there is not (none)	Es gibt, es gibt nicht (keine)	ess gipt, ess gipt nikht (keine)

I, you	Ich, Sie	ikh, zee
He, she	Er, sie	ehr, zee
We	Wir	veer
Mine, yours	Mein(e), Ihr(e)	mein(e), eer(e)
Ours, theirs	Unser, ihr	unzer, eer
At my place, At your place	Bei mir zu Hause, bei Ihnen zu Hause	bei meer tsu howze, bei eenen tsu howze
Wet, dry	Nass, trocken	nahss, trokken
Old, new	Alt, neu	ahlt, noy
Pretty, ugly	Hübsch, nicht nett	hewbsh, nikht net
Much, few	Viel, wenige	feel, vaynige
How many? How much?	Wieviel	veefeel
Cheap, expensive	Billig, teuer	billikh, toyer
Very expensive	Sehr teuer	zayer toyer
Free (of charge)	Umsonst	umzonst
More, less	Mehr, weniger	mayr, vayniger
Cheaper, more expensive	Billiger, teurer	billiger, toyerer
Heavy, light	Schwer, leicht	shvehr, leikht

2

Now, at the same time as...	Yetzt, gleichzeitig mit...	yetst, gleikh-**tseit**ikh mit
During	Während	**vay**rent
Early, late	Früh, spät	frew, shpayt
Here, there	Hier, dort	heer, dort
Inside, outside	Drinnen, draussen	**drin**nen, **drow**ssen
Up (stairs), down (stairs)	Oben, unten	**oh**ben, **un**ten
To...	Zu... nach...	tsu..., nach...
Near, far	Nahe, weit	**nah**-e, veit
In front of	Vor	for
Behind (after)	Hinten (nach)	**hin**ten (nach)
Sky	Himmel	**him**mel
Sun, moon	Sonne, Mond	**zon**ne, mont
Stars	Sterne	**shteh**rne
Light, darkness	Licht, Dunkelheit	likht, **dun**kelheit
Heat, cold, warm	Heiss, kalt, warm	heiss, kahlt, vahrm
East, west	Osten, Westen	**ohs**ten, **ves**ten,
North, south	Norden, Süden	**nor**den, **syew**den
Rain, snow, wind	Regen, Schnee, Wind	**ray**gen, shnay, vint

Earth, mountain, valley	Erde, Berg, Tal	**ehr**de, **behr**k, tahl
River, bridge	Fluss, Brücke	fluss, **brew**ke
Desert, sand	Wüste, Sand	**vew**ste, zahnt
Sea, water, ship	See, Wasser, Schiff	zay, **vah**sser, shiff
Country, place	Land, Ort	lahnt, ort
City, village	Stadt, Dorf	shtat, dorf
Road, street	Strasse	**shtrah**sse
House, flat	Haus, Wohnung	howss, **voh**nung
Room, door	Zimmer, Tür	**tsim**mer, tewr
Key, lock	Schlüssel, Schloss	**shlews**sel, shloss
Wall, window	Wand, Fenster	vahnt, **fen**ster
Roof, steps	Dach, Treppen	dakh, **trep**pen
Kitchen, toilet	Küche, Toilette	**kew**khe, twah**lette**
Bed, pillows	Bett, Kissen	bet, **kis**sen
Blanket, carpet	Bettdecke, Teppich	**bet**decke, **tep**pikh
Table, chair	Tisch, Stuhl	tish, shtool
Man, woman	Mann, Frau	mahn, frow
Father, mother	Vater, Mutter	**fah**ter, **mut**ter

4

English	German	Pronunciation
Son, daughter	Sohn, Tochter	zohn, tokhter
Grandson, granddaughter	Enkel, Enkelin	enkel, enkelin
Brother, sister	Bruder, Schwester	bruder, shvester
Uncle, aunt	Onkel, Tante	onkel, tahnte
Husband, wife	Ehemann, Ehefrau	ayemahn, ayefrow
Boy, girl	Junge, Mädchen	yunge, maydkhen
Old man, old woman	Alter Mann, alte Frau	ahlter mahn, ahlte frow
To want	Wünschen	vewnshen
I want, You want	Ich wünsche, Sie wünschen	ikh vewnshe, zee vewnshen
I wanted, you wanted	Ich wünschte, Sie wünschten	ikh vewnshte, zee vewnshten
I will want, you will want	Ich werde wünschen, Sie werden wünschen	ikh vehrde vewnshen, zee vehrden vewnshen
I do not want	Ich wünsche nicht	ikh vewnshe nikht
To visit	Besuchen	bezookhen
I visit, you visit	Ich besuche, Sie besuchen	ikh bezookhe, zee bezookhen
I visited, you visited	Ich besuchte, Sie besuchten	ikh bezookhte, zee bezookhten
I will visit, you will visit	Ich werde besuchen, Sie werden besuchen	ikh vehrde bezookhen, zee vehrden bezookhen

To speak	Sprechen	shpraykhen
I speak, you speak	Ich spreche, Sie sprechen	ikh sphraykhe, zee shpraykhen
I spoke, you spoke	Ich sprach, Sie sprachen	ikh sprach, zee shprakhen
I will speak, you will speak	Ich werde sprechen, Sie werden sprechen	ikh vehrde shpraykhen, zee vehrden shpraykhen
I do not speak	Ich spreche nicht	ikh shpraykhe nikht
To understand	Verstehen	fershtayen
I understand, you understand	Ich verstehe, Sie verstehen	ikh fershtaye, zee fershtayen
I understood, you understood	Ich verstand, Sie verstanden	ikh ferstahnt, zee fershtahnden
I do not understand	Ich verstehe nicht	ikh fershtaye nikht
To go	Gehen	gayen
I go, you go	Ich gehe, Sie gehen	ikh gaye, zee gayen
I went, you went	Ich ging, Sie gingen	ikh gink, zee gingen
I will go, you will go	Ich werde gehen, Sie werden gehen	ikh vehrde gayen, zee vehrden gayen
I do not go	Ich gehe nicht	ikh gaye nikht
To travel	Reisen	reizen
I travel, you travel	Ich reise, Sie reisen	ikh reize, zee reizen

I travelled, you travelled	Ich reiste, Sie reisten	ikh reiste, zee reisten
I will travel, you will travel	Ich werde reisen, Sie werden reisen	ikh vehrde reizen, zee vehrden reizen
I do not travel	Ich reise nicht	ikh reize nikht
To stand	Stehen	shtayen
I stand, you stand	Ich stehe, Sie stehen	ikh shtaye, zee shtayen
I stood, you stood	Ich stand, Sie standen	ikh shtahnt, zee shtahnden
I will stand, you will stand	Ich werde stehen, Sie werden stehen	ikh vehrde shtayen, zee vehrden shtayen
I do not stand	Ich stehe nicht	ikh shtaye nikht
To sleep	Schlafen	shlahfen
I sleep, you sleep	Ich schlafe, Sie schlafen	ikh shlahfe, zee shlahfen
I slept, you slept	Ich schlief, Sie schliefen	ikh shleef, zee shleefen
I will sleep, you will sleep	Ich werde schlafen, Sie werden schlafen	ikh vehrde shlahfen, zee vehrden shlahfen
I do not sleep	Ich schlafe nicht	ikh shlahfe nikht
To rest	Ruhen	roo-en
I rest, you rest	Ich ruhe, Sie ruhen	ikh roo-e, zee roo-en

I rested, you rested	Ich ruhte, Sie ruhten	ikh **roo**te, zee **roo**ten
I will rest, you will rest	Ich werde ruhen, Sie werden ruhen	ikh **vehr**de **roo**-en, zee **vehr**den **roo**-en
I do not rest	Ich ruhe nicht	ikh **roo**-e nikht
To eat	Essen	**essen**
I eat, you eat	Ich esse, Sie essen	ikh **esse**, zee **essen**
I ate, you ate	Ich ass, Sie assen	ikh **ahss**, zee **ahssen**
I do not eat	Ich esse nicht	ikh **esse** nikht
To drink	Trinken	**trinken**
I drink, you drink	Ich trinke, Sie trinken	ikh **trinke**, zee **trinken**
I drank, you drank	Ich trank, Sie tranken	in trank, zee **tranken**
I will drink, you will drink	Ich werde trinken, Sie werden trinken	ikh **vehr**de **trink**en, zee **vehr**den **trink**en
I do not drink	Ich trinke nicht	ich trink nikht
To be afraid	Angst haben	**ahnkst hahben**
I am afraid, you are afraid	Ich habe Angst, Sie haben Angst	ikh **hah**be ahnkst, zee **hah**ben ahnkst

I was afraid, you were afraid	Ich hatte Angst, Sie hatten Angst	ikh hatte ahnkst, zee hatten ahnkst
I will be afraid	Ich werde Angst haben	ikh vehrde ahnkst hahben
You will be afraid	Sie werden Angst haben	zee vehrden ahnkst hahben
I am not afraid	Ich habe keine Angst	ikh hahbe keine ahnkst
To sit	Sitzen	zitsen
I sit, you sit	Ich sitze, Sie sitzen	ikh zitse, zee zitsen
I sat, you sat	Ich sass, Sie sassen	ikh zahss, zee zahssen
I will sit, you will sit	Ich werde sitzen, Sie werden sitzen	ikh vehrde zitsen, zee vehrden zitsen
To hurry	Eilen, sich beeilen	eilen, zikh be-eilen
I am in a hurry	Ich bin in Eile	ikh bin in eile
You are in a hurry	Sie sind in Eile	zee zint in eile
I hurried, you hurried	Ich eilte, Sie eilten	ikh eilte, zee eilten
I will hurry, you will hurry	Ich werde eilen, Sie werden eilen	ikh vehrde eilen, zee vehrden eilen
I am not in a hurry	Ich habe keine Eile	ikh hahbe keine eile

I ask for help	Ich brauche Hilfe	ikh **browkhe** hilfe
You ask for help	Sie brauchen Hilfe	zee **browk**hen hilfe
I asked for help	Ich bat um Hilfe	ikh **baht** um hilfe
You asked for help	Sie baten um Hilfe	zee **bahten** um hilfe
I am not asking for help	Ich brauche keine Hilfe	ikh **browkhe keine hi**lfe
Passport	Pass	pahss
Flight	Flug	flook
Outgoing flight	Abgehender Flug	**ahp**-gayender flook
Following flight	Nächster Flug	**next**er flook
Flight number	Flugnummer	flook **noo**mer
Suitcase	Gepäck	ge**peck**
Customs	Zoll	tsol
Money	Geld	gelt

FIRST MEETING; GREETINGS	BEKANTMACHEN, BEGRÜSSUNGEN	BEKAHNTMAKHEN, BEGREWSSUNGEN
Hello!	Guten Tag	gooten tahk
Good morning	Guten Morgen	gooten morgen
Good evening	Guten Abend	gooten ahbent
Good night	Gute Nacht	goote nakht
Welcome!	Willkommen	villkommen
My name is ...	Ich heisse...	ikh heisse
I am from the United-States	Ich bin aus den Vereinigten Staaten	ikh bin owss dayn fehr-einikten shtahten
I speak only English	Ich spreche Englisch	ikh shpraykhe aynglish
I am pleased to meet you	Sehr angenehm	zayer ahngenaym
How are you?	Wie geht es Ihnen?	vee gayt es eenen?
Fine, thank you.	Danke, gut	dahnke, goot
How are things?	Was gibt's Neues?	vahss gipts noyess?
All right	Alles in bester Ordnung	ahless in bester ordnung

English	German	Pronunciation
I've come to learn about your country	Ich möchte Ihr Land kennen lernen	ikh **merkh**te eer lahnt **ken**nen **lehr**nen
I've come on a vacation	Ich bin auf Urlaub	ikh bin owf **ur**lowp
Is there someone here who speaks English?	Ist hier jemand, der Englisch spricht?	ist heer **yay**mahnt dehr **ayng**lish shprikht?
Yes, no	Ja, nein	yah, nein
I don't speak German	Ich spreche kein Deutsch	ikh **shpray**khe kein doytsh
I speak English	Ich spreche Englisch	ikh **shpray**khe aynglish
I speak a little	Ich spreche etwas	ikh **shpray**khe etvahss
Do you understand me?	Verstehen Sie mich?	fehr**shtay**en zee mikh?
I understand a little	Ich verstehe etwas	ikh fehr**shtay**e etvahss
Pardon, excuse me	Verzeihung	fehr**tsei**-ung
I am sorry	Ich bedaure	ikh be**dow**re
It doesn't matter	Macht nichts	makht nikts
Thank you very much	Vielen Dank	**fee**len dahnk
What do you want?	Was wünschen Sie?	vahss **vewn**shen zee?
I would like to visit the city	Ich möchte die Stadt besichtigen	ikh **merkh**te dee shtat be**zikh**tigen

12

English	German	Pronunciation
Wait a minute!	Warten Sie einen Moment!	vahrten zee einen moment!
Come with me!	Kommen Sie mit!	kommen zee mit!
I have to leave now	Ich muss jetzt gehen	ikh muss yetst gayen
Thank you for your attention	Vielen Dank für Ihre Aufmerksamkeit	feelen dahnk fewr eere owfmerkzahmkeit
Good luck!	Alles Gute	ahless goote
Goodbye!	Auf Wiedersehen!	owf veederzayn!

HOTEL

English	German	Pronunciation
I am looking for a good hotel	Ich suche ein gutes Hotel	ikh zookhe ein gootes hotel
I am looking for an inexpensive hotel	Ich suche ein billiges Hotel	ikh zookhe ein billiges hotel
I booked a room here. Is it ready?	Ich habe hier ein Zimmer bestellt, Ist es bereit?	ikh hahbe heer ein tsimmer beshtelt ist ess bereit?
Have you a single room? A double room?	Haben Sie ein Einzelzimmer? Doppelzimmer?	hahben zee ein eintsel tsimmer? doppel tsimmer?

English	German	Pronunciation
Have you a better room?	Haben Sie ein besseres Zimmer?	hahben zee ein besseres tsimmer?
Is the room air-conditioned?	Hat das Zimmer eine Klimaanlage?	hat dahss tsimmer eine kleema-ahnlahge?
Does the room have a shower?	Hat das Zimmer eine Dusche?	hat dahss tsimmer eine dooshe?
With breakfast?	Mit Frühstück?	mit frewshtik?
How much is the room?	Wieviel kostet das Zimmer?	veefeel kostet dahss tsimmer?
I should like to see the room	Ich möchte das Zimmer sehen	ikh merkhte dahss tsimmer zayen
Do you have something bigger? Smaller? Cheaper? Quieter?	Haben Sie etwas grösseres? Kleineres? Billigeres? Ruhigeres?	hahben zee etvahss grersseres? ...kleineres? billigeres? roo-igeres?
Will you send my bags to the room?	Können Sie mein Gepäck bringen lassen?	kernen zee mein gepeck bringen lahssen?
I would like to keep this in the safe	Ich möchte das im Safe aufbewahrt haben	ikh merkhte dahss im sayf owfbevahrt hahben
Where is the ladies' room? The men's room?	Wo ist die Damentoilette? Die Herrentoilette?	voh ist dee dahmen twahlette? ...dee hehren twahlette?

14

Where is the dining room?	Wo ist der Speisesaal?	voh ist dehr **shpeize**-zahl?
T.V. Room?	Der Fernsehraum?	dehr **fehrn**zay-rowm?
Please, wake me at ...	Wecken Sie mich bitte um...	**vecken** zee mikh **bitte** um...
Who's there? Please wait!	Wer ist da? Einen	vehr ist dah? **einen**
Come in!	Augenblick! Herein!	**owgenblick!** heh-**rein!**
May I have another towel?	Kann ich noch ein Handtuch	kahn ikh nokh ein **hant-**
	bekommen?	tookh be**kommen?**
May I have another pillow?	Kann ich noch ein	kahn ikh nokh ein **kopf-**
	Kopfkissen bekommen?	kissen be**kommen?**
...another blanket?	...noch eine Decke?	...nockh ein **decke?**
...hangers?	...Kleiderbügel?	**...kleider-bewgel?**
...hot water bottle?	...Wärmflasche	...**vehrm**-flahshe?
...night lamp?	...Nachtlampe	...**nakht**-lahmpe?
...thread and needle?	...Nadel und Faden	...**nah**del unt **fahden?**
...writing paper? pen?	...Schreibpapier? Feder?	...**shreib**-pahpeer? **fayder?**
Could you cable abroad for	Können Sie für mich ein	**kernen** zee fewr mikh ein
me?	Telegramm ins Ausland	tele**grahm** inss **owslahnt**
	schicken?	**shicken?**

A vacant room	Ein freies Zimmer	ein **frei-ess tsimmer**
Receptionist	Der Empfangschef	dehr em**pfahngs**-shef
Chambermaid	Das Zimmermädchen	dahs **tsimmer**-maydkhen
Security Officer	Der Sicherheitsbeamte	dehr **zikh**erheits be-**ahm**te
Waiter	Der Kellner	dehr **kellner**
Dining room	Der Speisesaal	dehr **shpeize**-zahl
Reception room	Empfangshalle	em**pfangs**-hahle
	Foyer, Gesellschaftsraum	fwah-**yay**, ge**zell**shahftsrowm
Lift boy (Elevator boy)	Der Fahrstuhlführer	dehr **fahr**-shtool-fewrer
Room key	Zimmerschlüssel,	**tsimmer**-shlewssel,
Room number	Zimmernummer	**tsim**mernumer
Bed, blanket	Bett, Bettdecke	bet, **bet**-decke
Sheet	Laken	**lah**ken
Men's toilet	Herrentoilette	**hehr**en-twahlette
Ladies' toilet	Damentoilette	**dah**men-twahlette
Toilet paper	Toilettenpapier	twaletten pah**peer**

INFORMATION AT HOTEL	INFORMATION IM HOTEL	INFORMAHTSYOHN IM HOTEL
Is there a taxi station nearby?	Ist hier in der Nähe ein Taxistand?	ist heer in dehr **naye** ein taxi-shtahnt?
What is the telephone number?	Wie ist Ihre Telefonnummer?	vee ist **eere** tele**fohn**-numer?
How do I get to...?	Wie komme ich zu...?	vee **komme** ikh tsu...?
By bus?	Mit dem Autobus?	mit dehm **owtoh**-booss?
Where is the bus stop?	Wo ist die Autobus-haltestelle?	voh ist dee owtoh-booss **hahl**te-shtelle?
Where is the nearest post office?	Wo ist das nächste Postamt?	voh ist dahss **nexte** post-ahmt?
Ladies' hairdresser	Damenfriseur	**dahmen**-freezerr
Barber	Herrenfriseur	**hehren**-freezerr
Laundry, shop	Wäscherei, Geschäft	**vesherei, gesheft**
Where can I get a snack?	Wo kann ich einen leichten Imbiss bekommen?	voh kahn ikh einen **leikhten imbiss** bekommen?
Is there a grocery nearby?	Ist hier in der Nähe ein Lebensmittelgeschäft?	ist heer in dehr **naye** ein **laybens**-mittel-gesheft?

English	German	Pronunciation
Where is the Tourist Information Office?	Wo ist das Auskunftsbüro für Touristen?	voh ist dahss **owsskunfts**-bewroh fewr **turisten**?
Can I have a programme of this week's events?	Kann ich das Unterhaltungsprogramm von dieser woche haben?	kahn ikh dahss **unter**-ahltungs-prograhm fon **deezer vokhe hahben**?
How can I get to	Wie kann ich zu... kommen?	vee kahn ikh tsu... **komm**en?
... on foot?	...zu Fuss?	...tsu fooss?
... by bus?	... mit dem Autobus?	mit dehm **ow**toh-booss?
... to this address?	...zu dieser Adresse?	...tsu **deezer** adresse?
... to the center of town?	...ins Stadtzentrum?	...inss **shtat**-tsentrum?
... to the shopping district?	...ins Geschäftsviertel?	...inss ge**shefts**-feertel?
... to a bookshop?	...zu einer Buchhandlung?	...tsu einer **bookh**hahntlung?
... to the market?	...zum Markt?	...tsum mahrkt?
... to the exhibitions?	...zur Austellung?	...tsur **owss**-shtellung?
... to the museum?	...zum Museum?	...tsum moo**zayum**?
... to the theatre?	...zum Theater?	...tsum ta**yah**ter?
... to the cinema?	...zum Kino?	...tsum **kee**no?
... to a nightclub?	...zum Nachtklub?	...tsum **nakht**-kloop?

What plays are running this week?	Was gibts es diese woche im Theater?	vahss gipts **deeze vokhe** im tayahter?
Which films worth seeing are on this week?	Welche Filme lohnte es sich diese Woche zu sehen?	**velkhe filme** lohnt ess zikh **deeze vokhe** tsu **zayen**?
Is there a tennis court nearby?	Ist hier in der Nähe ein Tennisplatz?	ist heer in dehr **naye** ein **tennis-plahts**?
Have you got any mail for me?	Haben Sie Post für mich bekommen?	**hahb**en zee post fewr mikh **bekomm**en?
Is there a message for me?	Ist eine Mitteilung für mich angekommen?	ist **eine mit**-teilung fewr mikh **ahn**-gekommen?
I am going out and will return at …	Ich gehe jetzt weg und komme um... wieder	ikh **gaye** yetst veck unt **komme** um ... veeder
I'll leave the hotel tomorrow at …	Ich verlasse das Hotel morgen um...	ikh fehr-**lahsse** dahss hotel **morg**en um...
Please make up my bill	Machen Sie mir bitte die Rechnung fertig	**makh**en zee meer **bitte** dee **rekh**nung **fehr**tikh
May I store my luggage here until …?	Kann ich mein Gepäck bis... hierlassen?	kahn ikh mein **gepeck** biss... **heer**lahssen?
Goodbye	Auf Wiedersehen	owf **veeder**zayn

TAXI

Please call me a taxi.	Bestellen Sie mir bitte ein Taxi	**beshtellen** zee meer **bi**tte ein **ta**xi
Driver would you please bring my suitcase inside?	Fahrer, bringen Sie mir bitte meinen Koffer herein	**fah**rer, **bring**en zee meer **bi**tte **mei**nen **koff**er heh-**rein**
Take me to this address, please ...	Bringen Sie mich bitte zu dieser Adresse	**bring**en zee mikh bitte tsu **dee**zer **a**dresse
Please drive more slowly	Fahren Sie bitte langsamer	**fah**ren zee bitte **lahng** zahmer
How much is the fare?	Was kostet die Fahrt?	vahss **kostet** dee fahrt?
Can you come here at ... in order to take me back?	Können Sie mich hier um... Uhr wieder abholen?	**kern**en zee mikh heer um... oor **vee**der **ahp**-hohlen?

IN THE POST OFFICE   IM POSTAMT   IM POST-AHMT

Where is the post office?	Wo ist das Postamt?	voh ist dahss **post**-ahmt?
Where can I send an overseas cable?	Von wo kann ich ein Überseetelegramm schicken	fon voh khan ikh ein **ewb**erzay-tele**grahm shick**en?
Please, give me an overseas cable form	Geben Sie mir bitte ein Formular für ein Überseetelegramm	**gay**ben zee meer bitte ein formew**lahr** fewr ein **ewb**erzay-tele**grahm**

20

English	German	Pronunciation
How much do I have to pay?	Was kostet das?	vahss **kostet** dahss?
What stamps do I need for this letter by ordinary mail?	Was für Marken brauche ich für diesen Brief mit gewöhnlicher Post?	vahss fewr **mahrken browk**he ikh fewr **deezen** breef mit ge**vern**likher post?
...by air mail?	...mit Flugpost?	...mit **flookpost**?
...by registered mail?	...eingeschrieben?	...**ein**geshreeben?
...by express delivery?	...express?	...**express**?
Please send this registered	Schicken Sie dies bitte eingeschrieben	**shick**en zee deess **bitte ein**geshreeben
Give me airletters to Europe, America, please	Geben Sie mir bitte Luftpostbriefe nach Europa, Amerika	**gayb**en zee meer **bitte luft**post-**bre**efe nach oy**rohp**a, a**may**reeka
Where is the nearest post box	Wo ist der nächste Briefkasten?	voh ist dehr **next**e breef-**kah**sten?
May I have some telephone tokens, please?	Kann ich bitte einige Fernsprechmünzen bekommen?	kahn ikh bitte einige **fehrn**-shpraykh-**mewnt**sen bekommen?

English	German	Pronunciation
Please, could you get me this number, as I could not get it by dialing?	Können Sie mich bitte mit dieser Nummer verbinden? Ich konnte sie bei direkter Wahl nicht erreichen.	kernen zee mikh bitte mit deezer numer fehrbinden? ikh konte zee bei deerekter vahl nikht ehr-reikhen
Please, could you put me through to the International Exchange for this number?	Können Sie mich bitte durch die internationale Telefonzentrale mit dieser Nummer verbinden?	kernen zee mikh bitte doorkh dee internahtsyohnahle telefohn tsentrahle mit deezer numer fehrbinden?
Please book me a call for tomorrow at ...	Ich möchte ein Gespräche für morgen um...	ikh merkhte ein geshpraykh fewr morgen um... ahn-melden
How much do I have to pay?	Was bin ich schuldig?	vahss bin ikh shuldikh?
Please, may I have a receipt?	Kann ich bitte eine Quittung bekommen?	kahn ikh bitte eine kvittung bekommen?
Thank you, goodbye	Danke, auf Wiedersehen	dahnke, owf veederzayn

22

IN THE RESTAURANT	IM RESTAURANT	IM RESTOHRAHNT
I am hungry	Ich bin hungrig	ikh bin **hung**rikh,
I am thirsty	Ich bin durstig	ikh bin **door**stikh
Where is there a good restaurant?	Wo ist hier ein gutes Restaurant?	voh ist heer ein **goo**tes restoh**rahnt**?
Waiter, Waitress	Kellner, Kellnerin	**kell**ner, **kell**nerin
Can I see the menu?	Kann ich die Speisekarte sehen?	kahn ikh dee **shpeize**-kahrte **za**yen?
Breakfast, Lunch	Frühstück, Mittagessen	**frew**shtick, **mit**tahk-essen
Dinner	Abendbrot	**ah**bent-broht
I would like to order	Ich möchte bestellen	ikh **merkh**te be**shtel**len
Give me this	Geben Sie mir das	**gay**ben zee meer dahss
Tea with lemon, tea with milk	Tee mit Zitrone, Tee mit Milch	tay mit tsit**roh**ne, tay mit milkh
Coffee and milk, Turkish coffee	Kaffee mit Milch, Türkischer Kaffee	kah**fay** mit milkh, **tewr**kishe kah**fay**
Nescafé and milk	Neskaffee mit Milch	neska**fay** mit milkh
Milk, cocoa, espresso	Milch, Kakao, Expresso	milkh, kah**kow**, ex**presso**

Cold, warm, hot	Kalt, Warm, Heiss	kahlt, vahrm, heiss
Cold water, soda water	Kaltes Wasser, Sodawasser	kahltes vahsser, zohdavahsser
Orange juice, grapefruit juice	Apfelsinensaft, Pampelmusen saft	ahpfelzinen-zaft pahmpelmoozen-zaft
Cake, ice-cream	Kuchen, Eis	kookhen, eis
White beer, black beer	Bier, Malzbier	beer, mahlts-beer
Sweet wine, dry wine	Süsswein, herber Wein	zewss-vein, hehrber vein
Cognac, whisky, arak	Kognac, Whisky, Arrak	konyahk, viskee, ahrahk
Buttered roll	Brötchen mit Butter	brertkhen mit buter
Roll and margarine	Brötchen mit Margarine	brertkhen mit margareene
White bread, black bread	Weissbrot, Schwarzbrot	veissbroht, shvahrts-broht
Toast and jam	Toast mit Marmelade	tohst mit mahrmelahde
Rolls	Brötchen	brertkhen
Egg, soft-boiled egg	Ei, weiches Ei	ei, veikhes ei
Omelette, fried egg	Omelett, Setzei	omelet, zets-ei
White cheese, yellow cheese	Weisskäse, Gelber Käse	veis-kayze, gelbe kayze
Yogurt, sour-cream	Yoghurt, saurrahm	yogurt, zower-rahm

Sausage, hot dogs	Wurst, Würstchen	voorst, **vewrst**-khen
Vegetable salad	Gemüsesalat	**gemewze**-zahlaht
Salt, oil, sugar	Saltz, Öl, Zucker	zahlts, erl, tsuker
Pepper, lemon juice	Pfeffer, Zitronensaft	**pfeffer**, tsitrohnen-zaft
Olives, pickled cucumber	Oliven, saure Gurke	oh**leeven**, zowre goorke
Herring, pickled fish	Hering, eingelegter Fisch	**hehring**, eingelaykter fish
Smoked fish	Räucherfisch	roykher-fish
Bakala, filleted fish	Seehecht, Fischfilet	zayhekht, fish filay
Baked, filled carp	Gebacken, Gefüllter Karpfen	gebahken, gefilte karpfen
Baked, grilled, boiled	Gebacken, Gegrillt, Gekocht	gebahken, gegrilt, gekokht
Fried, steamed	Gebraten, Gedämpft	gebrahten, gedemft
Chicken, turkey, duck	Huhn, Pute, Ente	hoon, poote, ente
Beef, lamb	Rindfleisch, Lammfleisch	rintfleish, lahmfleish
Liver, tongue	Leber, Zunge	layber, tsunge
Steak, shnitzel	Steak, Schnitzel	stayk, shnitsel
Meat balls	Fleischklösschen	fleish-klerss-khen
Bean soup	Bohnensuppe	bohnenzuppe
Vegetable soup	Gemüsesuppe	gemewze-zuppe

English	Deutsch	Pronunciation
Chicken soup, meat soup	Hühnersuppe, Fleischsuppe	**hewner**-zuppe, **fleish**-zuppe
Mashed potatoes, Chips	Kartoffelbrei, Chips	**kartoffel**brei, chips
Fruit salad	Obstsalat	**opst**-zahlaht
Pudding, bavaria cream	Pudding, Bayerischer Krem	**pudding, bei**-erishe krem
Glass, bottle, cup	Glas, Flasche, Tasse	**glahss, flahshe, tahsse**
Spoon, fork, knife	Löffel, Gabel, Messer	**lerfel, gahbel, messer**
Plate, teaspoon	Teller, Teelöffel	**teller, tay**-lerfel
Serviette, ashtray	Serviette, Aschenbecher	**zervee-ette, ah**shen-bekher
Toothpicks	Zahnstocher	**tsahn**-shtokher
How much must I pay?	Was habe ich zu zahlen?	vahss **hahbe** ikh tsu **tsahlen?**
Change and a receipt, please	Bitte den Rest und eine Quittung	**bitte** dehn rest unt **eine kvit**tung

GROCERY / LEBENSMITTEL-GESCHÄFT / LAYBENS-MITTEL-GESHEFT

English	Deutsch	Pronunciation
White bread, brown bread	Weissbrot, Graubrot	**veiss**broht, **grow**broht
Milk, yogurt	Milch, Yoghurt	milkh, **dicke** milkh, **yogurt**
Sour cream, white cheese	Sauerrahm, Weisskäse	**zower**-rahm, **veiss**-kayze

English	German	Pronunciation
Yellow cheese, salt cheese	Gelber Käse, Salzkäse	gelber kayze, zahlts-kayze
Butter, margarine, oil	Butter, Margarine, Öl	buter, margahreene, erl
Sardines, tuna fish	Sardinen, Thunfisch,	zardeenen, toonfish,
Tuna salad	Thunfischsalat	toonfish-zahlaht
Olives, eggs	Oliven, Eier	oleeven, eier
Soup mix	Suppenpulver	zuppen-pulfer
Sugar, honey, salt	Zucker, Honig, Salz	tsucker, honikh, zahlts
Preserved meat	Konserviertes Fleisch	konzehrveertes fleish
Soap	Waschseife	vash-zeife
Flour, noodles	Mehl, Nudeln	mayl, noodeln
Please give me	Geben Sie mir bitte	gayben zee mir bitte
How much does...cost?	Was kostet...?	vahss kostet...?

FRUITS AND VEGETABLES

OBST UND GEMÜSE

OHPST UNT GEMEWZE

English	German	Pronunciation
Almonds	Mandeln	mahndeln
Apples	Äpfel	epfel
Apricot	Aprikose	ahpreekohze

27

Banana	Banane	banahne
Beans	Bohnen	bohnen
Beetroot	Rote Rübe	rohte rewbe
Cabbage	Kohl	kohl
Carrot	Mohrrübe, Karotte	mohr-rewbe, kahrotte
Cauliflower	Blumenkohl	bloomenkohl
Corn	Mais	meiss
Cucumber	Gurke	goorke
Dates	Datteln	dahteln
Eggplant	Aubergine, Eierfrucht	ohbehrzheene, eier-frukht
Figs	Feigen	feigen
Garlic	Knoblauch	knoplowkh
Grapefruit	Pampelmuse	pahmpelmooze
Grapes	Weintrauben	veintrowben
Lemon	Zitrone	tsitrohne
Lettuce	Kopfsalat	kopfzahlaht
Squash	Kürbis	kewrbis
Melon	Melone	melohne

Nuts	Nüsse	**new**sse
Onion	Zwiebel	**tsvee**bel
Oranges	Orangen (Apfelsinen)	o**rahn**zhen, (**ahp**felzinen)
Peaches	Pfirsiche	**pfeer**zikhe
Pears	Birnen	**beer**nen
Peas	Erbsen	**ehr**psen
Pepper	Pfeffer	**pfeffer**
Pomegranate	Granatapfel	gra**naht**-**ahp**fel
Potatoes	Kartoffeln	kar**toffeln**
Radish	Rettich	**rett**ikh
Rice	Reis	reis
Spinach	Spinat	shpi**naht**
Tomatoes	Tomaten	to**mah**ten
Watermelon	Wassermelone	**vah**ssermelohne

BANK	**BANK**	**BANK**
Where is the nearest bank?	Wo ist die nächste Bank?	voh ist dee nexte bank?
I have dollars to exchange.	Ich habe Dollars zu wechseln	ikh hahbe dollars tsu vekseln
Travellers checks.	Reiseschecks	reize-shecks
Will you please change...	Wechseln Sie mir bitte...	vekseln zee meer bitte ...
dollars into local currency	Dollars in hiesige	dollars in heezeege
for me?	Währung um	vayrung um
Could I have it in small	Könnte ich es bitte in	kernte ikh es bite in
change, please?	Kleingeld haben?	kleingelt hahben?
... in large notes?	...in grossen Scheinen?	...in grohssen sheinen?
Could you, please, give me	Können Sie mir bitte diesen	kernen zee meer bitte deezen
change for this note?	Schein wechseln?	shein vekseln?
Cash, checks	Bargeld, Schecks	bahrgelt, shecks
Clerk, manager	Beamter, Direktor	be-ahmter, direktor
Cash desk, cashier	Kasse, Kassierer	kahsse, kaseerer

CLOTHES	KLEIDER	KLEIDER
I would like to buy...	Ich möchte kaufen	ikh **merkh**te **kow**fen
My size is ... My number is ...	Meine Grösse ist..., meine Nummer ist...	meine **groh**sse ist..., meine **numer** ist...
May I try it on?	Kann ich es anprobieren?	kahn ikh es **ahn**-proh**beer**en?
This is too short, too long	Das ist zu kurz, zu lang	dass ist tsu koorts, tsu lahng
It is too narrow, too wide	Das ist zu eng, zu weit	dahss ist tsu eng, tsu veit
I would like to have it shortened	Ich möchte es Kürzer gemacht haben	ikh **merkh**te es **kewrt**ser ge**makht hah**ben
A pair of shorts	Ein Paar Shorts	ein pahr shorts
A pair of trousers	Ein Paar Hosen	ein pahr **hoh**zen
Boots	Stiefel	**shtee**fel
Brassiere	Büstenhalter	**bews**ten-**hah**lter
Button	Knopf	knopf
Cape	Cape	kayp
Coat	Mantel	**mahn**tel
Collar	Kragen	**krah**gen
Cotton material	Baumwollstoff	**bowm**-vol-shtoff

Dress	Kleid	kleit
Gloves	Handschuhe	**hahnt**-shoo-e
Hat	Hut	hoot
Handkerchief	Taschentuch	**tah**shen-tookh
Jacket	Jackett	zhah**ket**
Ladies' handbag	Damenhandtasche	**dah**men-hahnt-tahshe
Leather	Leder	**lay**der
Linen	Leinen	**leinen**
Nylon stockings	Nylonstrümpfe	nylon-**shtrewmpfe**
Night shirt	Nachthemd	**nakht**-hemt
Pocket	Tasche	**tah**she
Pantyhose	Strumpfhose	sht**rumpf**-hohze
Pajamas	Pyjama (Schlafanzug)	pi**zhah**ma, **shlahf**-ahntsuk
Raincoat	Regenmantel	**raygen**-mahntel
Robe	Morgenrock	**morgen**rock
Rubber boots	Gummistiefel	**goo**mi-shteefel
Sandals	Sandalen	zan**dah**len
Scarf	Schal	shahl
Scissors	Schere	**shayre**

32

Shoe laces	Schnürsenkel	**shnewr-zenkel**
Shoes	Schuhe	**shoo-e**
Silk	Seide	**zeide**
Shirt	(Herren-) Hemd	**(hehren-) hemt**
Slippers	Hausschuhe (Pantoffeln)	**howss-shoo-e, (pantoffeln)**
Sports shoes, sneakers	Sportschuhe,	**shport**shoo-e
Stockings	Strümpfe	**shtrewmpfe**
Sweater	Sweater, Pullover	**svetter, pull**over
Swimsuit	Badeanzug	**bah**de-ahn-tsuk
Suit	Anzug	**ahn**-tsuk
Synthetic material	Synthetischer Stoff	**zewntay**tisher shtoff
Belt	Gürtel	**gewrtel**
Tie	Krawatte, Schlips	**kravah**te, shlips
Umbrella	Regenschirm	**raygen**-sheerm
Underpants	Unterhose	**un**terhohze
Velvet	Samt	**zahmt**
Undershirt, vest	Unterhemd, Weste	**un**terhemt, **ves**te
Woolen material	Wollstoff	**vol**shtoff
Zipper	Reissverschluss	**reiss**-fehr-shluss

COLORS	**FARBEN**	**FAHRBEN**
I want a light shade	Ich möchte eine helle	ikh merkhte eine helle
Dark shade	Schattierung . dunkle	hateerung, dunkle
	Schattierung	shateerung
Red, yellow	Rot, Gelb	roht, gelp
Green, blue	Grün, Blau	grewn, blow
Purple, gray	Lila, Grau	leelah, grow
Black, white	Schwarz, Weiss	shvarts, veiss
Brown, pink	Braun, Rosa	brown, rohza

LAUNDRY	**WÄSCHEREI**	**VESHEREI**
Could you please clean my suit, coat, sweater?	Können Sie mir bitte den Anzug reinigen? Den Mantel? Den Sweater?	kernen zee meer bitte den ahn-tsuk reinigen? den mahntel? den svetter?
Please, could you wash and iron the shirts and underwear for me?	Können Sie mir bitte die Hemden und die Unterwäsche waschen und bügeln?	kernen zee meer bitte dee hemden unt dee unterveshe vahshen unt bewgeln?

English	German	Pronunciation
When will they be ready for me?	Wann ist das fertig?	vahn ist dahss **fehr**tikh?
Please also do any necessary repairs	Bessern Sie bitte auch alles, was nötig ist, aus	**bessern** zee bitte owkh **ahless vahss nertikh ist**
The belt of the dress is missing	Der Kleidergürtel fehlt	dehr **kleidergewrtel faylt**

AT THE HAIR DRESSER

BEIM FRISEUR

BEIM FREEZERR

English	German	Pronunciation
I want to get a hair cut	Ich möchte die Haare geschnitten haben	ikh **merkh**te dee **hahre geshnitten hahben**
In front, on the sides, behind	Vorn, an den Seiten, hinten	forn, ahn den **zeiten, hin**ten
Shorter, longer	Kürzer, länger	**kewrt**ser, **len**ger
Side locks, beard, moustache	Seitenlocken, Bart, Schnurrbart	**zeitenloken**, bahrt **shnurbahrt**
How long must I wait?	Wie lange habe ich zu warten?	vee **lahn**ge **hah**be ikh tsu **vahr**ten?
A short while, a long time	Nicht lange, lange	nikht **lahn**ge, **lahn**ge
I want a shampoo, please	Ich möchte den Kopf gewaschen haben	ikh **merkh**te den kopf **gevahshen hahben**

English	German	Pronunciation
The water is too hot	Das Wasser ist zu heiss	dahss **vahss**er ist tsu heiss
I want a shave	Ich möchte mich rasieren lassen	ikh **merkh**te mikh rah**zeer**en **lahs**sen
Be careful here!	Vorsicht hier!	**for**zikht heer!
I want my hair dyed	Ich möchte das Haar färben lassen	ikh **merkh**te dahss hahr **fehr**ben **lahs**sen
I want my hair set	Ich möchte das Haar legen lassen	ikh **merkh**te dahss hahr **layg**en **lahs**sen
Pedicure, Manicure	Pediküre, Maniküre	paydi**kew**re, mahni**kew**re

BOOKSHOP / BUCHHANDLUNG / BOOKH-HANDLUNG

English	German	Pronunciation
I would like to buy ...	Ich bitte um...	ikh bitte um...
...A newspaper	..eine Zeitung	...eine **tseit**ung
...A magazine	...eine Zeitschrift	...eine **tseit**shrift
...A guidebook	...einen Reiseführer	...einen **reize**-fewrer
...A map of the city	...einen Stadtplan	...einen **shtat**plahn
...A map of the country	...eine Landkarte	...eine **lahnt**-karte
...Envelopes	...Briefumschläge	...**breef**-umshlayge
...A writing pad	...einen Schreibblock	...einen **shreib**-block

...A pencil	...einen Bleistift	...einen **blei**-shtift
...A fountain pen	...einen Füllfederhalter,	...einen **fewlfayder**-hahlter
...A ballpoint pen	...einen Kugelschreiber	...einen **koogelsh**reiber
...A refill for the pen	...eine Ersatzmine	...eine **ehrzahts**-meene

THE WEATHER	DAS WETTER	DAHS VETTER
What a beautiful day!	So ein schöner Tag!	zoh ein **sherner** tahk!
Bright, the sun is shining	Hell, die Sonne scheint	hell, dee **zonne** sheint
Warm, hot, very hot	Warm, heiss, sehr heiss	vahrm, heiss, **zayer** heiss
Chilly, cold, very cold	Eisig, kalt, sehr kalt	**eizikh**, kahlt, **zayer** kahlt
Dry, heat wave	Trocken, Hitzewelle	**trocken**, hitse-velle
Damp, drizzle, rain	Feucht, Nieselregen, Regen	foykht, **neezel**-raygen, **raygen**
Cloudy, foggy	Bewölkt, Neblig	**bevelkt**, **nayblikh**
To wear a warm coat	Einen warmen Mantel tragen	einen **vahrmen mahn**tel trahgen
Raincoat, cape	Regenmantel, Cape	**raygen**mahntel, keyp
Rubber boots	Gummistiefel	**goo**mi-shteefel
To take an umbrella, Parasol	Einen Regenschirm	einen **raygen**-sheerm
	nehmen, Sonnenschirm	**naymen**, **zonnen**-sheerm

37

TRANSPORT	VERKEHR	FEHRKAYR
Bus, train, plane	Autobus, Zug, Flugzeug	**ow**toh-booss, tsook, **flook**-soyk
Underground, express train	Untergrundbahn, Schnellzug	**untergrunt**bahn, **shnell**tsoog
Ticket	Fahrkarte,	**fahr**karte,
Ticket office	Fahrkartenschalter	**fahr**kartenshalter
Driver, steward, stewardess	Fahrer, Steward, Stewardess	**fahrer**, **steward**, **steward**ess
Load/luggage, porter	Gepäck, Gepäckträger	**gepeck**, **gepeck**trayger
Where is the lost baggage office?	Wo ist das Fundbüro für verlorenes Gepäck?	voh ist dahss **funtbewro** fewr fehrlohrenes **gepeck**?
I left ... in the coach	Ich habe... im Wagen liegen lassen	ikh **hahbe**... im **vahgen** **leegen lahssen**

TRAIN, BUS

	ZUG, EISENBAHN, AUTOBUS	TSOOK, EIZENBAHN, OWTOH-BOOSS
When does the train for ... leave?	Wann geht der Zug nach... ab?	vahn gayt dehr tsook nakh... ahp?
How do I get there?	Wie Komme ich dorthin?	vee **komme** ikh dort-hin?

38

By train, bus, underground (subway)	Mit dem Zug, mit dem Autobus, mit der Untergrundbahn?	mit dem tsook, mit dem òwtoh-booss, mit dehr untergruntbahn?
Where is the ticket office?	Wo ist der Fahrkartenschalter?	voh ist dehr fahrkartenshalter?
At what time does the next train leave for ...?	Um wieviel Uhr geht der nächste Zug nach... ab?	um veefeel oor gayt dehr nexte tsook nakh... ahp?
Give me a ticket for ... please	Eine Karte nach..., bitte!	eine kahrte nach..., bitte
If possible, by the window and facing the front	Möglichst am Fenster und in Fahrtrichtung	merglikhst ahm fenster und in fahrt-rikhtung
Where can I find a porter?	Wo ist ein Gepäckträger?	voh ist ein gepecktrayger?
Please, take the bags to the coach	Bringen Sie bitte das Gepäck zum Wagen	bringen zee bitte dahss gepeck tsum vahgen
Where is the dining coach?	Wo ist der Speisewagen?	voh ist dehr shpeize-vahgen?
May I open (close) the window?	Kann ich das Fenster öffnen (schliessen)?	kahn ikh dahss fenster erfnen (shleessen)?
May I smoke?	Darf ich rauchen?	dahrf ikh rowkhen?
When does the train arrive at?	Wann kommt der Zug in... an?	vahn komt der tsook in... ahn?

What bus goes to...?	Welcher Autobus geht nach...?	velkher owtohbooss gayt nakh...?
Where is the bus to ...?	Wo steht der Autobus nach...?	von shtayt der owtohbooss nakh...?
How much is a ticket to ...?	Was kostet eine Karte nach...?	vahss kostet eine karte nakh...?
Is this the bus to ...?	Ist das der Autobus nach...?	ist dahss der owtohbooss nakh...?
I am looking for this address	Ich suche diese Adresse (Anschrift)...	ikh zookhe deeze adresse (ahn-shrift)...
At which station do I get off?	Sagen Sie mir bitte, wo ich aussteigen muss	zahgen zee meer bitte voh ikh ows-shteigen muss

AIRPLANE

FLUGZEUG

FLOOKTSOYKH

| By which means of transport do I get to the airport? | Mit welchem Verkehrsmittel komme ich zum Flugplatz? | mit velkhem fehrkayrsmittel komme ikh tsum flookplahts? |
| Is there a bus service (taxi) to there? | Fahren Autobusse (Taxis) dorthin? | fahren owtohboosse (taxis) dort-hin? |

40

English	German	Pronunciation
When will I be picked up?	Wann werde ich Abgeholt?	vahn **vehr**de ikh **ahp**-geholt?
Which is the nearest bus stop to the airport?	Wo ist die nächste Autobus-haltestelle zum Flugplatz?	voh ist dee **nexte** owtohbooss-halte-shtelle tsum **flook**-plahts?
When should I be there?	Wann muss ich dort sein?	vahn muss ikh dort zein?
At what time does the plane take off?	Wann geht das Flugzeug?	vahn gayt dahss **flook**-tsoykh?
When will it arrive?	Wann kommt es an?	vahn komt dahss ahn?
Is there a flight to?	Gibt es einen Flug nach...?	gipt es einen flook nakh...?
What is the flight number?	Wie ist Die Flugnummer?	vee ist dee **flook**numer?
I have nothing to declare	Ich habe nichts zu deklarieren	ikh **hah**be nikts tsu deklahreeren
This is all I have	Das ist alles, was ich habe	dahss ist **ah**less, vahss ikh **hah**be
Please, take my luggage	Nehmen Sie bitte mein Gepäck	**nay**men zee bitte mein **ge**peck
May I have a travel sickness pill, please?	Kann ich eine Tablette gegen Reiseübelkeit bekommen?	**kahn ikh eine** tablette **gay**gen **reize**-ewbelkeit bekommen?

41

English	German	Pronunciation
May I have a glass of water?	Kann ich ein Glas Wasser bekommen?	kahn ikh ein glahss **vahs**ser bekommen?

CAR JOURNEY

English	German	Pronunciation
Where can I rent a car?	Wo kann ich ein Auto mieten?	voh kahn ikh ein **owtoh meet**en?
I have an international driving license	Ich habe einen internationalen Führerschein	ikh **hah**be einen internatsyo-**nah**len fewrershein
How much is it to rent a car per day?	Was kostet die Miete für ein Auto pro Tag?	vahss kostet dee **meete** fewr ein owtoh proh tahk?
What is the additional rate per kilometer?	Wass kostet jedes zusätzliche Kilometer?	vahss kostet yaydes **tsu**-zetslikhe kilometer?
Where is the nearest petrol (gas) station?	Wo ist die nächste Tankstelle?	voh ist dee **nexte tahnk**shtelle?
Please, put in ... liters	Füllen Sie bitte... Liter ein	**fewlen** zee bitte... **liter** ein
Check the oil, please	Prüfen Sie bitte den Ölstand	**prewf**en zee bitte den erlshtahnt
...the brakes	...die Bremsen	...dee **brem**zen
...the gear box	...die Gänge	...dee **gaynge**

AUTOFAHRT — **OWTOH-FAHRT**

English	German	Pronunciation
Please put water in the battery	Füllen Sie bitte den Akkumulator mit Wasser	fewlen zee bitte den ahkoomoolahtor mit vahsser
...in the radiator	...den Radiator	...dehn radiahtor
Change the oil in the car, please	Wechseln Sie bitte das Motoröl in Auto aus	vekseln zee bitte dahss motohr-erl im owtoh owss
May I have a road map of the area?	Kann ich eine Autokarte von dieser Gegend bekommen?	kahn ikh eine owtohkarte fon deezer gaygent bekommen?
Please, inflate the tires, the reserve wheel, too	Pumpen Sie bitte die Reifen auf, auch das Reserverad	pumpen zee bitte dee reifen owf, owkh dahss rayzerve-rahd
Please repair the puncture	Reparieren Sie bitte die Panne	raypahreeren zee bitte dee pahne
Please change the inner tube, the tire	Wechseln Sie bitte den Reifenschlauch aus	vekseln zee bitte dehn reifen-shlowkh owss
What is the speed limit?	Was ist die Höchstgeschwindigkeit?	vahss ist dee herkhst-geshvindikh-keit?
Which is the way to ...?	Wie fährt man nach...?	vee fahrt man nakh...?
Is that a good road?	Ist die strasse gut?	ist dee shtrahsse goot?

Is there a shorter way?	Gibt es einen Kürzeren Weg?	gipt es einen **kewrts**eren veck?
Which place is this?	Welcher Ort ist hier?	**vel**kher ort ist heer?
Is this the road to ...?	Ist das der Weg nach?	ist dahss dehr veck nakh...?
Yes, no	Ja, Nein	yah, nein
Please, go back	Fahren Sie bitte zurück	**fah**ren zee bitte tsu**rewk**
Go straight on	Fahren Sie weiter geradeaus	**fah**ren zee **vei**ter gerahde-owss
Turn to the right (left)	Biegen Sie rechts (links) ein	**bee**gen zee rekhts (links) ein
Turn to the north, (south, east, west)	Halten Sie sich nördlich, (südlich, östlich, westlich)	**hal**ten zee zikh **nerd**lik (**zewd**likh, **erst**likh, **vest**likh)
This way	Hier entlang!	heer ent**lahng**
That way	Dort entlang!	dort ent**lahng**
How far is it to ...?	Wie weit ist es bis...?	vee veit ist es bis...?
Is it near? (far?)	Ist es nah? (Weit?)	ist es nah? (veit?)
Very far?	Sehr weit?	**zay**er veit?
There, here	Dort, hier	dort, heer

English	German	Pronunciation
Please show me on the map	Zeigen Sie mir das bitte auf der Karte	**tseigen** zee meer dahss **bitte** owf dehr **kahr**te
Where are we?	Wo sind wir?	voh zint veer?
Where is the place that we want to go to?	Wo ist der Ort, zu dem wir hinwollen?	voh ist der ort tsu dehm veer **hin**vollen?
On which road should we travel?	Welche Strasse sollen wir nehmen?	**velk**her **shtrahsse** **zollen** veer **nay**men?
Take this road	Nehmen Sie diese Strasse!	**naymen** zee **deezer shtrahsse**

TRAFFIC SIGNS / SCHILDER / SHILDER

English	German	Pronunciation
Stop!	Halt!	halt!
Caution!	Vorsicht!	**for**zikht!
Dangerous curve	Gefährliche Kurve	ge**fehr**likhe **koor**ve
Slow!	Langsam!	**lahng**-zahm
Danger!	Gefahr!	ge**fahr**
First Aid	Erste Hilfe	**ehr**ste **hil**fe
Red Cross	Rotes Kreuz	**roh**tes **kroyts**
Pharmacy	Apotheke	ahpo**tay**ke

45

Police	Polizei	**politsei**
No parking	Feuerlöscher	**foyer-lersher**
No entry	Eintritt verbotten	**eintritt fehrbohten**
No crossing	Überqueren verboten	**ewber-kvehren fehrbohten**
One-way Street	Einbahnstrasse	**einbahn -shtrahsse**
Pedestrain crossing	Fussgängerübergang	**fewss-gaynger-ewber-gahng**
Detour	Umweg, Umleitung	**umveck, umleitung**
Men at work	Bauarbeiten!	**bow-ahrbeiten**
Right	Rechts	**rekhts**
Left	Links	**links**
Entrance	Eingang	**eingahng**
Exit	Ausgang	**owssgahng**
No smoking	Rauchen verboten!	**rowkhen fehrbohten**
Information	Auskunft	**owskunft**
W.C. (water-closet)	Toiletten	**twahletten**
Men's toilet	Männer (Herren)	**menner (hehren)**
Ladies'toilet	Frauen (Damen)	**frowen (dahmen)**

English	German	Pronunciation
Crossroad, junction	Querstrasse, Kreuzung	kvehrshtrahsse, kroytsung
Bridge	Brücke	brewke
Highway	Landstrasse	lahnt-shtrahsse
Bad road	Schlechte Strasse	shlekhte shtrahsse
Narrow road	Schmale Strasse	shmahle shtrahsse
Road under repair	Wegarbeiten!	veck-ahrbeiten
Steep incline	Steiler Abhang	shteiler ahp-hahng
Steep decline	Abschüssiger Weg	ahp-shewsiger veck
Sharp turn	Scharfe Kurve	sharfe koorve
Children on the road	Kinder auf der Strasse	kinder owf dehr shtrahsse

GARAGE

GARAGE, AUTOWERKSTATT

GARAZHE, AUTOHVERKSHTATT

English	German	Pronunciation
Where is a garage nearby?	Wo ist eine Garage in der Nähe?	voh ist eine garazhe in dehr naye?
Please check and adjust the brakes	Bitte die Bremsen zu prüfen und in Ordnung zu bringen	bitte dee bremzen tsu prewfen unt in ordnung tsu bringen

English	German	Pronunciation
Please check the gearbox and adjust the clutch	Bitte die Gänge zu prüfen und die Kupplung einzustellen	bitte dee gaynge tsu prewfen unt dee kuplung ein-tsu-shtellen
The engine uses too much oil	Der Motor verbraucht zu viel Öl	dehr motohr fehrbrowkht tsu feel erl
The engine is overheating	Der Motor wird zu heiss	dehr motohr veert tsu heiss
The radiator needs refilling too often	Das Wasser im Radiator verbraucht sich zu schnell	dahss vahsser im radiahtor fehrbrowkht zikh tsu shnell
Please check the plugs	Prüfen Sie bitte die Zündherzen	prewfen zee bitte dee tsindhertsen
Please check the points	Prüfen Sie bitte die Kontakte	prewfen zee bitte dee kontakte
The car doesn't start well	Der Motor springt schwer an	dehr motohr shpringt shvehr ahn
Please check the headlight alignment	Prüfen Sie bitte den Scheinwerfer	prewfen zee bitte dehn sheinvehrfer

REPAIRS	REPARATUREN	REPARATOOREN
Wheel balance	Rädereinstellung	rayder-einshtellung
Oil change	Ölwechsel	erl-veksel
Tighten screws	Schrauben anziehen	shrowben ahn-tsee-en
Fill the radiator	Den Radiator auffülen	dehn radiahtor owf-fewlen
Oil the engine	Den Motor ölen	dehn motohr erlen
Wheel alignment	Rädereinstellung	rayder-einshtellung
Water for the battery	Wasser für den Akku	vahsser fewr dehn ahkoo
The gear is stuck	Der Gang ist stecken geblieben	dehr gahng ist shtecken gebleeben
The oil is leaking	Das Öl tropft	dahss erl tropft
The part is burnt out	Der Teil ist verbrannt	dehr teil ist fehrbrahnt
To take a wheel apart	Ein Rad auseinandernehmen	ein raht owsseinander-naymen
Short circuit	Kurzschluss	kurts shluss
The steering wheel is loose	Das Steuerrad ist locker	dahss shtoyer-raht ist locker
The axle rod is broken	Die Achsenstange ist gebrochen	dee ahksen-shtahnge ist gebrokhen
Puncture in the tire	Eine Reifenpanne	eine reifen-pahne
Everything is O.K.	Alles in Ordnung	ahless in ordnung

PARTS OF A CAR	AUTOTEILE	OWTOH-TEILE
Battery	Batterie, Akku	batteree, ahkoo
Brakes	Bremsen	bremzen
Carburetor	Vergaser	fehrgahzer
Clutch	Kupplung	kupplung
Distilled water	Destilliertes Wasser	destileertes vahsser
Filter	Filter	filter
Gear	Gang	gahng
Ignition	Zündung	tsewndung
Lubrication	Ölung	erlung
Pedal	Pedal	paydahl
Piston	Kolben	kohlben
Radiator	Radiator, Kühler	radiahtor, kewler
Spark plugs	Zündkerzen	tsewnt-kehrtsen
Spring	Feder	fayder
Steering wheel	Steuerrad	shtoyer-raht
Wheel, wheels	Rad, Räder	raht, rayder

50

PHYSICIANS	ÄRZTE	EHRTSTE
Where does an English speaking doctor live?	Wo wohnt ein Arzt, der Englisch spricht?	voh vohnt ein ahrtst, dehr aynglish shprikht?
I need first aid	Ich brauche erste Hilfe	ikh browkhe ehrste hilfe
Can you recommend a good doctor?	Können Sie einen guten Arzt empfehlen?	kernen zee einen gooten ahrtst empfaylen?

TYPES OF DOCTORS	SPEZIALÄRZTE	SHPETSYAHL-EHRTSTE
Ear, nose and throat specialist	Hals-, Nasen- und Ohrenarzt	hahlss nahzen unt ohrren-ahrst
Orthopedist	Orthopäde	ortoh-payde
Surgeon	Chirurg	khiroorg
Pediatrician	Kinderarzt	kinder-ahrtst
Gynecologist	Gynaekologe, Frauenarzt	gewnaykolohge, frowen-ahrtst
Dermatologist	Dermatologe, Hautarzt	dermatolohge, howt-ahrtst

Eye specialist	Augenarzt	owgen-ahrtst
Neurologist	Neurologe	noyrolohge
Internal specialist	Internist	interneest
Dentist	Zahnarzt	tsahn-ahrtst

ILLNESSES	**KRANKHEITEN**	**KRAHNK**-HEITEN
I have no appetite	Ich habe keinen Appetit	ikh **habe keinen** ahpeteet
Nausea	Übelkeit	ewbelkeit
Infection	Infektion	infekts**yohn**
Depression	Depression	daypress**yohn**
Cold	Erkältung	ehr**keltung**
Vomiting	Erbrechen	ehr**braykhen**
Pregnancy, pregnant	Schwangerschaft, schwanger	**shvanger**shaft, **shvahng**er
Contraction	Erkrankung	ehrkrahnkung
Heart patient	Herzkranke(r)	**hehrts**-krahnker
Fever	Fieber	feeber

PARTS OF THE BODY	KÖRPERTEILE	KERPER-TEILE
Ankle, appendix	Fussknöchel, Blinddarm	**fooss**-knerkhel, **blint**dahrm
Arm, artery	Arm, Schlagader	ahrm, **shlahk**-ahder
Back, bladder	Rücken, Blase	**rew**ken, **blah**ze
Blood, bone	Blut, Knochen	bloot, **kno**khen
Breast, chest	Brust, Brustkasten	broost, **broost**kahsten
Ear, elbow	Ohr, Ellbogen	ohr, **ell**bohgen
Eye, eyes	Auge, Augen	**ow**ge, **ow**gen
Finger	Finger	**finger**
Foot, feet	Fuss, Füsse	fooss, fewsse
Gland	Drüse	**drew**ze
Hand, head	Hand, Kopf	hahnt, kopf
Heart, heel	Herz, Ferse	hehrts, **fehr**ze
Hip	Hüfte	**hewf**te
Intestine	Darm, Eingeweide	dahrm, **ein**geveide
Joints, kidney	Gelenke, Niere	**gelehn**ke **neere**
Knee, leg	Knee, Bein	knee, bein
Liver	Leber	**lay**ber
Lungs, mouth	Lungen, Mund	**lun**gen, munt

Muscle	Muskel	**mooskel**
Neck	Hals (Genick)	hahlss (**genick**)
Nerve, nerves	Nerv, Nerven	nehrf, **nehrfen**
Nose	Nase	**nahze**
Palm	Handfläche,	**hahnt**-flekhe
Rib	Rippe	**rippe**
Shoulder	Schulter	**shoolter**
Skin	Haut,	howt
Spine	Rückgrat	**rewk**-graht
Stomach,	Magen	**mahgen**
Throat	Kehle	**kayle**
Thumb	Daumen,	**dowmen**
Tongue	Zunge	**tsunge**
Tonsil	Mandel,	**mahndel**
Tooth, teeth	Zahn, Zähne	tsahn, tsayne
Urine	Urin	oo**reen**
Vein	Vene	**vay**ne

PHARMACY	APOTHEKE	AHPOTAYKE
Where is the nearest pharmacy?	Wo ist die nächste Apotheke?	voh ist dee nexte ahpotayke?
Which pharmacy is on duty tonight?	Welche Apotheke hat heute Nachtdienst?	velkhe ahpotayke hat hoyte nakht-deenst?
Have you a medicine for a headache?	Haben Sie ein Mittel gegen Kopfschmerzen?	hahben zee ein mittel gaygen kopf-shmehrtsen?
Iodine, aspirin	Iod, Aspirin	yohd, aspireen
Valerian drops	Baldriantropfen	bahldriahn-tropfen
Antiseptic cream	Antiseptische creme	antizeptishe kraym
Hot water bottle	Wasserflasche	vahsser-flahshe
Cottonwool	Watte	vahte
Thermometer	Thermometer	tehrmometer
I need first aid	Ich brauche erste Hilfe	ikh browkhe ehrste hilfe
What are the office hours?	Wann ist dort offen?	vahn ist dort offen?

TIME	**ZEIT**	**TSEIT**
What is the time?	Wieviel Uhr ist es?	veefeel oor ist es?
It is four o'clock	Es ist vier Uhr	es ist feer oor
Five minutes past six	Fünf (Minuten) nach sechs	fewnf (minooten) nakh zeks
Half past five	Halb sechs	hahlp zeks
A quarter past seven	Viertel nach sieben,	feertel nakh zeeben
Ten minutes to eight	Zehn (Minuten) vor acht	tsayn (minooten) for akht
Morning, midday, afternoon	Morgen, Mittag, Nachmittag	morgen, mittahk, nakhmittahk
Evening, night, midnight	Abend, Nacht, Mitternacht	ahbent, nakht, mitternakht
Today	Heute	hoyte
Yesterday	Gestern	gestern
The day before yesterday	Vorgestern	forgestern
Tomorrow	Morgen	morgen
The day after tomorrow	Übermorgen	ewbermorgen
A second, hour	Eine Sekunde, Eine	eine zekunde, eine
quarter of an hour	Stunde, Viertelstunde	shtunde, feertel-shtunde
Half an hour	Eine halbe Stunde	eine hahlbe shtunde
Forty minutes	Vierzig Minuten	feertsikh minooten

Day, days, week, weeks	Tag, Tage, Woche, Wochen	tahk, tahge, vokhe, vokhen
Month, months, year, years	Monat, Monate, Jahr, Jahre	mohnaht, mohnahte, yahr, yahre
Period of ... years, in a month	Zeit von... Jahren, In einem Monat	tseit fon... yahren, in einem mohnaht
Early, I am early	Früh, ich bin früh dran	frew, ikh bin frew drahn
Late, I am late	Spät, ich bin zu spät gekommen	shpayt, ikh bin tsu shpayt gekommen

DAYS OF THE WEEK — WOCHENTAGE — VOKHEN-TAHGE

Sunday, Monday	Sonntag, Montag	zontahk, montahk
Tuesday, Wednesday	Dienstag, Mittwoch	deenss-tahk, mittvokh
Thursday, Friday	Donnerstag, Freitag	donnerss-tahk, freitahk
Saturday	Sonnabend (Samstag)	zonahbent (zahmss-tahk)

57

MONTHS	MONATE	MOHNAHTE
January, February	Januar, Februar	yahnuahr, februahr
March, April, May	März, April, Mai,	mehrts, apreel, mei
June, July, August	Juni, Juli, August	yoonee, yoolee, owgoost
September, October	September, Oktober	september, oktohber
November, December	November, Dezember	november, detsember

SEASONS	JAHRESZEITEN	YAHRES-TSEITEN
Spring, Summer	Frühling, Sommer	frewling, zommer
Autumn, Winter	Herbst, Winter	hehrpst, vinter

NUMBERS	ZAHLEN	TSAHLEN
One, two	Eins, zwei	einss, tsvei
Three, four	Drei, vier	drei, feer
Five, six	Fünf, sechs	fewnf, zeks
Seven, eight	Sieben, acht	zeeben, akht
Nine, ten	Neun, zehn	noyn, tsayn

58

Eleven, twelve	Elf, zwölf	elf, tsverlf
Thirteen, fourteen	Dreizehn, vierzehn	**dreits**ayn, **feert**sayn
Fifteen, sixteen	Fünfzehn, sechzehn	**fewnft**sayn, **zekh**-tsayn
Seventeen, eighteen	Siebzehn achtzehn	**zeeb**tsayn, **akht**-tsayn
Nineteen, twenty	Neunzehn, zwanzig	**noynt**sayn, **tsvahn**tsikh
Twenty-one	Einundzwanzig	**ein**-unt-**tsvahn**tsikh
twenty-two	Zweiundzwanzig	**tsvei**-unt-**tsvahn**tsikh
Thirty, forty	Dreissig, vierzig	**dreis**sikh, **feert**sikh
Fifty, sixty	Fünfzig, sechzig,	**fewnft**sikh, **zekh**-tsikh,
Seventy	Siebzig	**zeeb**tsikh
Eighty, ninety	Achtzig, neunzig,	**akht**-tsikh, **noynt**sikh,
One hundred	Hundert	**hoon**dehrt
One hundred and one	Hunderteins	**hoon**dehrt-einss
Two hundred	Zweihundert	**tsvei**-hoondehrt
One thousand	Tausend	**tow**zent
One thousand and one	Tausendeins	**tow**zent-einss
Two thousand	Zweitausend,	**tsvei**-towzent
Two thousand and one	Zweitausendeins	**tsvei**-towzent-einss
One million, one billion	Eine Million, eine Milliarde	eine mil**yohn**, eine mil**yahrde**

EMERGENCY EXPRESSIONS	AUSDRÜCKE FUR EINE NOTLAGE	OWSS-DREWKE FEWR EINE NOHTLAH-GE
Help!	Hilfe!	**hil**fe!
Thief!	Diebe!	**dee**be!
Stop, thief!	Fasst den Dieb!	fahst dayn deeb!
Don't touch me!	Nicht anrühtrn!	nikht **ahn**rewren!
Leave me alone!	Lassen Sie mich in Ruhe!	**lah**ssen zee mikh in **roo**-e!
Call the police!	Rufen Sie die Polizei!	**roo**fen zee dee poli**tsei**!
I've lost my way.	Ich habe mich verirrt.	ikh **hah**be mikh fehr-**eert.**
How do I get to this address?	Wie komme ich zu dieser Adresse?	vee **kom**me ikh tsu **dee**zer a**dresse**?
I don't feel well.	Mir ist schlecht!	meer ist shlekht!
Call a doctor!	Rufen Sie einen Arzt!	**roo**fen zee **ei**nen artst!
Call a taxi!	Bestellen Sie ein Taxi!	be**shtell**en zee ein **ta**xi!
Take me to a first-aid station.	Bringen Sie mich zur Erste-Hilfse-Station.	**bring**en zee mikh tsur **ehr**ste-**hilf**e-shtahts**yohn.**
Take me to the hospital.	Bringen Sie mich in ein Krankenhaus.	**bring**en zee mikh in ein **krahnk**en-howss.
Take me to a doctor.	Bringen Sie mich zu einem Arzt.	**bring**en zee mikh tsu **ei**nem artst.